FLESH IN THE INKWELL: POEMS FROM A WRITER'S LIFE

ॐ

Flesh in the Jnkwell:
poems from a writer's life

Winona Baker

leaf press

b3400 3848

Library and Archives Canada Cataloguing
in Publication

Baker, Winona, 1924-
    Flesh in the inkwell : poems from a
writer's life / Winona Baker.

Poems.
ISBN 978-1-926655-09-3

    I. Title.

PS8553.A3855F54 2010   C811'.54
C2010-900758-1

We are grateful to the artist for permission to use
the cover image: Catherine Heard, *Untitled,* 2010
© CARCC, 2010.

Catherine Heard is represented by Edward Day
Gallery in Toronto: www.edwarddaygallery.com

A sincere thank you also to Helen Baker for the
author's photograph.

Leaf Press
Box 416
Lantzville, B.C. Canada
V0R 2H0 www.leafpress.ca

PS
8753
.A415
F54
2010

for my adult children and their best beloveds

ॐ

Flesh in the Inkwell: poems from a writer's life

You should write only when, each time you dip your quill in the inkwell, you leave in it a piece of flesh.

Lev Nikolaevich Tolstoy

Problem Child

"Who taught you all that, doctor?" "Poverty."
Albert Camus

Sometimes I answer her knock
A waif with needs and long face
waits on my WELCOME mat

Mingled odours from fringe-farm animals
chickens   cows   drift into the room

Her small hands rake badly cut hair
In hand-me-downs hardly worth washing
she snuffles. October to May
her throat and ears ache

Don't want
this timid bookwormish dreamer
with picked-up manners
parroting phrases she hopes will please
smiling at people whose cupboards are full

who feels damned
for something she can't remember doing and
goes like a stone where kicked

a girl
who thinks people who aren't poor
have no problems

The Beginning that Began My Ending

I too, no doubt, am an accident of timing,
like a million others ... Gwendolyn MacEwen

Conception is possible
during daylight hours but
I imagine beginning
one Presbyterian night

when my parents lived
in a prairie town, in the best house
my mother would have in her life

a house with bedrooms
before the weeping times

There's never a perfect time
or place to be conceived
but why didn't I wait
for more auspicious stars
linger longer in bardo
or get in a line headed
PEOPLE WHO WANT BABIES

I wasn't hurt when Mother said
she didn't want any more
Who'd want six children
(none of us twins)
in eight and a half years?

He wouldn't consider condoms—
said they were against nature

Old wives told her breast feeding
was a form of birth control
Another one said tell him
Have all the fun you want
in the front parlour, but—
go back in the kitchen to spit

That June night in Saskatchewan
did Mother go tired to bed after
breast-feeding my red-headed sister?

I imagine Mother lying
in the missionary position

When he finished
she'd get up to douche
while his Celtic sperm
swarmed toward her Loyalist egg

ॐ

Embedded in Her Inner Landscape

*Some people believe unborn souls choose their
own parents.* Eden Robinson

Egged-in a womb-room
behind a woman's soft walls
before becoming a mammal
I lollygaggled about

Did I dream it would last forever?
Hear mother tell eight-year-old Freida
You're the oldest—have to help me
Added nanny to her chores

Making my way
up the evolutionary ladder
I tested the five senses
wiggled things as they sprouted

Speechless—I mouthed
before-being-born languages
slurps, chirps, squeaks, grunts

When baby Beth howled
did I hear Mother tell Father
Freida needs her sleep?

Then a baritone voice: *Come,
daddy will sing a tune
for his red-headed lassie*

Aroman Yinnan Voyuch
the Gaelic folk song
he sang to all the babies

The Naming

... we arrive here improvised ...
Wislawa Szymborska

I entered the world of light—gasped
Air rushed into my lungs

Jesus, Sappho—what sinners or saints
had some of their particles in that first holy breath
that made me a mammal?

Such blooming confusion
a buzzing babble disordered senses

filled with sweet and milky
snuggled on something warm
skin touching dewed permeable skin

Bobbling head scanned
the hospital room   white   white
curlicued iron bed
lace-curtained window
filled with drifting whiteness

Caresses on my bare back
suddenly stopped—softness tensed
I burrowed in

Footsteps—not those of the nurse
who sometimes entered our room
A cold and pungent someone
with a voice from my piscine life
Well Winnie, another bonnie lass

We relaxed
You don't mind—our fifth girl?
Wanted our last to be a boy
a brother for Hector

Let's have a look
daddy cradled me to his chest
She'll be Winnifred—for you

No, she needs her own name
The air filled with words
Jemima   Isobel   Julia   Moneila ...

In my first school I taught a lovely Indian child—
was more strict with her than others
Didn't want Winona called 'teacher's pet'

Masquerade

*Photographic images are pieces of evidence
in an ongoing biography ...* Susan Sontag

I believed mother's story for years:

*When we lived in town
your father and I went
to a masquerade
on St. Patrick's Day*

*We had such a good time at the party
weren't home till well after midnight*

*We opened our front door
and there was a new-born baby
in the middle of the front room rug*

*Well—
we didn't need any more children
but you had a good head of hair
and were bonny—decided to keep you*

There are no baby pictures of me
I've one of costumed people
taken at a masquerade
the night before I was born

Before the Depression
Daddy came home and announced
Get ready to move

I've rented this house
bought a quarter section
about thirty miles north

Good soil, has a cabin
I'll make money on it
build us a better house

Getting to our new home was like
a rambling three-day picnic

Creaking wagons parted long grasses
I sat on bags and bundles
Older sisters and my brother
walked or rode horses as they
herded the cows along

Sometimes I was lifted—rode high
hugged by or hugging someone
or stared from Daddy's shoulders

A man so charming
that when we reached the farm
mother's tears and angry mutterings about no:
church, school, doctor, had slowed down

How to fit five children in a two-room cabin
Help with seeding—prepare for a prairie winter?

Marry the farmer, marry the farm

Back in Ontario what
would her Methodist mother think?

My Methodist Grandmother Visits

I first saw my maternal grandmother
when she stepped from the buggy
and kissed five grandkids aged two to ten

She looked over our two-room cabin
asked
—Where will I sleep?
—In the bedroom, mother
—Where will you and William sleep?
—In the barn

Was it that
or the long train trip from Ontario
in those untravelled times
that made her drop her head
on the table and sob

—You were one of our smart ones
had the education   you've come to this
five children in two rooms

And you've never been so thin!

Mommy said Daddy promised
a fine new house when the crop was in

Grandma dried her eyes, blew her nose
on a hankie with a tatted border
gave us each a maple sugar candy
and made some new rules

Threshers could no longer
crowd the house five times a day
Midmorning and midafternoon lunch
would be brought to the working field

Didn't she know Daddy made all the rules?

Photograph

A photo looks at you too. Richard Harrington

One prairie morning a friend of dad's
arrived at our quarter section
Whoa!

Pushed buffalo robes aside
leaped from sleigh to snow

*No, can't stay Bill—just dropped by
to show my new camera
and take a picture of your family*

Dad herded outside: my big brother
three sisters and two-year-old me—
still youngest

How long it took to capture
this bit of biography. Something
kept going awry with the camera

Weren't allowed to wait inside
we shuddered in freezing wind
blowing over endless whiteness

Told to have fun while waiting
ran in aching snow
stamped cold feet
lined up again and again

*Scots are hardy
take things like a man*

Stuffing freezing mittenless hands
in my armpits didn't warm them
I couldn't help crying

Five children
in a grainy black and white snapshot

I wear a bonnet on bowl-cut hair
in shrunken babyish knits
shudder   frozen-fisted   weep
in my first picture

ॐ

The Slough

I MAKING MUDPIES

In underpants mother made
from unbleached cotton flour sacks
I spent pre-school summers
playing by a prairie slough

I was two and Beth four
when six-year-old Anne took us there
It seemed to my eyes a lake

Anne dragged an apple crate down
Don't pester me Winona
there's a table—go play house

She read Burgess books for hours
We mixed clay and water
our bowls, dishes and babies
hardened in Saskatchewan sun

The friendly cows and Beauty—
Daddy's old horse put out to pasture
wandered down to drink
or rest in poplar shade

We peed and pooped there, wiped ourselves with leaves
softer than the pages of Eaton's catalogue

Before going home we ran naked into the slough
sloshed mud from ourselves and underpants
Anne finger combed our hair, herded us to a home
that seemed happy then

II BEAUTY

For bringing us the horse we could almost forgive you
for bringing us whiskey. Lame Deer

She was one of the horses that made the prairie more beautiful
Anne why is she always here when other horses are working?

Like Tommy's great-grandma who knits all day in her rocker
Beauty's too old to work anymore, but Daddy'll never send her away

Anne squatted by a stump, waved a handful of grass: *Here Beauty*
She came, lowered her head and my sister jumped on
The horse raised her head, Anne slid down her neck
then quickly flipped about face-forward ready to ride

Beth and I leaped about—*We wanna' ride Beauty too!*

You darn kids want to do everything that big kids do
You can't come—there's nobody here
to boost you up behind me

But our big brother came by with his Ranger 22
he wanted to show us his bounty of gopher tails
Hector lifted us, we rode Beauty
over the singing prairie
                    and Anne told a story

Once upon a time daddy had different neighbours
When the mother was ready to get her baby
she fell hard on ice—needed a doctor quick
The father put her in a sleigh and came for daddy's team
It was the best one because of Beauty

III THE BARQUE VERONICA

During long winters the livestock drank
from an Eaton's watering trough

After chinooks blew spring into Saskatchewan
the animals drank at the slough

Hector promised Dad he'd be careful
and still get chores done on time
if he could use the trough
for a boat in summer

Freida, Anne, Beth and I helped
drag its heaviness to the water

He announced
I'm christening her The Barque Veronica
after a ship Dad sailed on

This was my idea—so I'm captain
Nobody hoists anchor without me!

Water can be dangerous—
besides you could lose my oar

We shoved *The Veronica* in
scrambled aboard

I'm taking you on her maiden voyage
Hector poled us out to sea

IV Visitors

When I was three and Beth five
we went by ourselves to the slough
if Anne had to do chores

One mixing-mud afternoon I heard voices — stared
at Mommy, Daddy and Anne coming with four strangers

Elizabeth and Winona say hello to your Uncle Bert
Aunt Louise, Aunt Mamie — and here's your Cousin Dorrie

They were dressed like people in Eaton's catalogue
We gawked at: uncle's Panama hat, light suit
the aunties' flowered voile dresses

How smooth their silk stockings —
dust on Cuban-heeled shoes

Cousin Dorrie wore frilled dotted organdie
white socks and black patent shoes
hair in ringlets like a Shirley Temple doll
She pressed closer to Aunt Mamie

When Beauty nuzzled Daddy
he stroked the horse's face ... beamed

Beth and Nonie, wash-up and come to the house
He hoisted Anne on Beauty
Get Hector, he's hunting gophers

... don't worry Bert, she's safe riding bareback
If she falls, no stirrups to get caught in

I met Daddy's smiling eyes
I think he saw us brown and sturdy

met Mommy's eyes — anger   sadness
then something worse
shame

Dusk—saw Mommy slip out the back door
a chance to have her to myself
I ran out and caught her hand

Mother needs to be alone for awhile
Lip out   sulked backwards to the house
watched her walk toward our slough

Then quiet as a cat I trailed
to where poplars made stalking easier

Kept up when she ran because
she suddenly fell   scared
I peered through the gloom

She ran again—then flung herself like
I sometimes just flung my body on water
and hit the ground again
Go back! she'd said

I watched her strange game
Run   throw the body down
Run   throw the body down ...

When she staggered toward the house
I nearly ran to her

Years later I showed Mother my diaphragm
Teased: *Kids are nice, but I don't want eight*

She bristled
I tried everything
burning lysol douches ... and
do you remember the slough?
I ran around and around it—fell so hard
Nothing stopped you babies

VI A Word for Everything

My first Easter
mommy took me off her breast
said since I had some teeth
should learn to feed myself

The Easter bunny brought me eggs
in a white enamel bowl
It had a blue border and on the bottom
was an outlined-in-blue silhouette
of a cat, over the marks C A T

I greedily ate from my bowl: porridge, stew or slops—
made of bread, milk and a sprinkle of sugar
When I finished, there always, the cat sat

At the slough I tried forming a bowl
the sides wouldn't stay up so I flattened the mud
made a plate with a crooked cat in the middle
and bowl's marks beneath it

Anne said *Oh—you've printed the word cat*

Time stopped—thoughts raced through my head
some marks weren't just decorations
like auntie's cross-stitching on a runner

Anytime, anywhere, anyone saw the marks C A T
it was cat—then there must be a word for everything

VII WRITE IT DOWN

My fourth summer—
Beauty followed us into the slough
or did we bring her in, to get washed up too?
When we came out she stayed
Anne arrived—we coaxed and shoved

Father said latecomers should miss their supper
Beauty wouldn't come out of the slough

We followed him to the water; C'mon girl
She nickered   raised a foot, strained forward
swayed in the muddy place

Anne stay here—keep her quiet
Jim and Freida get to the neighbours
see if they can give a hand
The rest—double quick to the house

Winnie, keep the young ones inside

Mother put us to bed early
Don't keep asking the same question
She nursed Iainsie-boy, Babe-sey boy

I fell asleep while she read
a Burgess bedtime story

Woke to nightmare noises
Mommy wasn't beside us
Red curls together, Babe-sey boy and Beth slept sweetly
I wandered through the house, then outside
toward noise   lanterns   people

Roped all around   Beauty threshed the water
while the team and people tugged

Why wouldn't she just be quiet?
Hindquarters in muddy water
tried to rear   her head fell again

Dad handed Hector his gun
Shoot her

No! I won't!
She's never done anything to me!

William—don't ask our son!
Shut your face—
I'm making a man not a milksop!

I'm running forward screaming
Don't shoot her—just pull her out of the slough!

Christ Winnie—I told you, keep her in the house!

The neighbour, who didn't hunt, took the gun
Here Bill—let me

Mother pulled me to the house
It'll be all right now ...
Cry quiet then—you'll wake Beth and the baby

At the Senior's Lodge Mother looks out at snow
Reminds me of the prairie
people and animals lost in winter ...

summer had dangers too
We lost a horse in a slough ...

What? You girls never caused Beauty's death ...
besides she was old—horses could do that

Your father said I had the best hand
kept me up for hours. He told me
write it down—write what I say about Beauty

Going home the bus is held up at a truck stop
to let snow plows ahead

I walk by a field ringed by firs
in the middle of all the whiteness
one black horse

Cat Lives—Gophers

After Beauty died
Beth and I didn't want
to play by the slough anymore

We wandered around the farm
looking for someplace
to play house

Let's pretend we're gophers
We used our hands to hollow
a cave in an embankment

Played gophers there a few days
Let's add a tunnel

Stopped as we dug to look back
little streamers of sand
trickled down like water
through the dusty air

It's too hard digging by hand
I'm getting the coal shovel
Beth said as she backed out

A waterfall of sand
Drowning I struggled
tried to push the weight away

until it became so peaceful
I didn't care about anything

Somewhere Beth was screaming
Someone was shaking me   slapping
Wake up! Wake up now Nonie!

Obey your father ...
I opened my eyes

❦
Going, Going, Gone

The Depression, the drought—dad decided
We'll leave everything, move to the West Coast
There'll only be room in the Model T for camping gear
and a few clothes. You won't need heavy coats
B.C.'s the California of Canada

Auction day I was told *keep out of the way*
but don't run off. I stood among long legs as
a chanting man hammered away farm machines,
horses, cows, everything my parents owned
    Going   going   gone!

When things didn't sell or went for IOUs
Mother tried to look pleasant as more
men signed with an X and more
IOUs went into the money box

Dad paid the auctioneer, pocketed the cash,
put the round-as-a-baseball
roll of IOU's into his black sea chest

Eight people climbed into the Model T
little brother on Mother's lap in front
while five children vied for room
among boxes in the back seat

We waved away our farm
and when the Ford was going at top speed
played a made up game
wish-I-could-have-brought

My turn: rag doll, crayons—but first pick
papier mâché bunny: he came apart
showed where my Easter egg had been

Anne suddenly stared down at me
What are you hiding in your sweater?

She grabbed my bunny, flung him out in the rain
We were told no room for anything!

I quietly cried for miles, empty inside

Fire and Father

*The histories of families cannot be separated
from the histories of nations.* Susan Griffin

One cold Depression morning
Father opened the fire box of the stove
Before the clock struck six he shook down ashes
crushed newspapers, topped them with cedar kindling
slashed a wooden match across
the thigh of his patched overalls

Flames grew
He weaned them to hardwood split by Hector
His sleep-hungry son joined him in the kitchen

They neither smiled nor spoke
Father had captained ships—
commands were given once

They walked through the ashy dawn
to the barn where warm animals
father was fond of waited

Then Mother came out to the stove
sighing   unhuddled herself
bestirred herself   battered
the stiffened porridge to mush

Daughters drifted downstairs
Beth dressed two drowsy littles

Anne and Nonie ran
to the lanterned barn
threw fragrant armfuls in mangers

then rushed back to the stove
washed in a basin of kettle-warmed water

Beside the fire Anne sang to the baby
Good morning merry sunshine
How did you wake so soon?

Father came in—singing stopped
children stepped to the table
He sat at the head like the Scot
in a story Mother told
about a round table
Wherever that man sits
is the head of the table

As porridge went round in bowls
Mother tried conversations
(nobody mentioned her black eye)

There's a pheasant struts in the field
Hector, you're such a good shot
could you get him for supper?
Could use a fresh feather in my hat

Spoons scraped up porridge
Father fed the fire

Before He Ran Away

Mummy's screams rose in the night
slashed holes in our sleep.

On the haunted upstairs landing
Anne and Hector struggled.

Let   go   of   my   gun! he hissed.

Mummy could get between you.

I'm a crack shot
I'll blow Dad's damn brains out!

Don't!   Don't! she panted.
You'll hang in Oakalla!

You'll burn
in the fires of Hell forever!

Sleepers

Honeybees buzz in a sphere to keep warm in winter
moving from the inner warm to the outer cool position.

We seemed too many children to dream in one bed
Mother showed us how to sleep spoon-fashion
Biggest to smallest we curled knees
back of knees of the child ahead
Snugged   slept long nights
turned like birds changing patterns

When I needed to pee I wriggled out
careful not to disturb patched patchwork blankets
old coats cocooning warm air

Stooped   searched beneath
sagging bed slats praying pot
wouldn't be full   squatted   peed

Stood   found space at the edge
behind a curved back   slid in
hoped no sibling would say
Keep your cold feet off me

Dr. McBurney tapped
his Sphinxian way
making his annual visit
to our country school

When he sat in teacher's chair
his black-suited bulk overflowed
like burnt bread over a pan

Class, Dr. McBurney is here
to give you a free examination
If he finds something wrong
I will write it down
on this important form

Miss Shardrey mimed on the air
with her red MacLean's pen

Dr. McBurney will sign it
Carefully take it home and
give it to your father

They don't know what Daddy said
about their important form last year
Glasses? Can't be blind!
You're always reading!
Do you want to wear eye crutches?
You were acting the fool I bet!

He let Mummy read the form
then threw it in the fire

Teacher pulled on a ring
under the rolled-down map
the world slapped up like a blind—
a blackboard of blurred busywork
to do while the Doctor examined

Furtively we watched
wondered who'd be flawed
No hand waved for the outhouse
as through the chalky air
children moved to the front
called alphabetically—
everyone but me

Summoned last I warily
walked toward the desk.
Teacher nodded to the doctor—

metal in my ears
wood in my mouth
stethoscope on flat chest
Finished, I waited for the form

The doctor's eyes behind glasses
were pale-lashed as a pig's—
but I thought them kind
Bend your head over

I lowered my coward's head
fat fingers pulled my hair
this way and that
I must not   must not cry

Everyone will know—
the only one searched for head lice
I need no leper's bell

&.

Mary Murchison McLeod

How living are the dead! Florence Coates

Sometimes when mother was trying
to make a meal out of not much, or find
something we could wear to school
she'd angrily sigh, then say

If your grandmother was still alive
you girls would have a much better life

She didn't mean her mother
our faraway grandma in Ontario
She meant her mother-in-law
Mary Murchison McLeod
who died years before I was born

Wished mother wouldn't say that
the sentence usually signalled
a stressful soliloquy starting
She'd tell him ...

You have family now — before you make speeches
for Dr. Bethune in China, learn
how to talk to your own sons ...

Before you collect for brigades in Spain
make sure your children have something
to put in their lunch buckets ...

Sometimes I'd go alone
to the front room and stare
at Grandma's sepia portrait
in its large oval frame

Thought — if I gaze long enough
at her strong, calm face can I learn
how to make us a better life?

Apple Orchards of My Childhood

Their spring boughs flaunted far too many
clustered white pink-edged blossoms
After a fumbling of bees
the trees grew greenly practical

In early summer boys waged war
pockets full of nut-hard apples
Later I climbed with a book
listened—leaf music
read   ate apples

Fall: picked trees freighted with fruit
stored the best—hoped they'd keep till summer
Some escaped harvesting hands
joined plashed-down windfalls on the ground

When the winter tree's blackened twigs
were welded on a skim-milk sky
we lugged from the earthy cellar
Delicious, Northern Spies, Kings, Russets
colours of the autumn
Apples—
they seemed so Canadian
these immigrants from Persia

꙰

King Alfred and Me

Alone, secluded as a nun
except in another room
a baby lies, fern fingers curled
sweet against his sleeping cheek

Inside a skull a busy brain
computing undomestic questions
not: which detergent gives
the whitest diapers in this town
whether x @ 2 for y
is the supermart's best buy

While I bake I wonder what if
Napoleon had won those wars
What was Shakespeare really like

When King Alfred's army was routed
and pursued by Norse invaders
cotters gave him sanctuary

Alfred left alone one day
to mind cakes cooking on the hearth
instead became engrossed in planning
campaigns to win back his crown

(I burn my cakes like Alfred did)

In a Printed Housedress

She dances the tango

Cheek to air   arms taut   advances
on laced-up Cuban-heeled shoes

Stop   stamp stamp turn
who picked these partners?

One favours silence
uncluttered rooms
(she'd sooner talk to herself)
there are books to read and write

Loves her body best right after the bath
why can't it
always be this clean?

In printed housedress turns
She's washed
blood   sweat   semen
    from
her body   from others'

Giving care
she would suckle the world

Step back and   forward   turn
a woman   dances the tango

The Seeker

*It is only shallow people who do not judge
by appearances.* Oscar Wilde

Seeking beauty, the woman
imagines a tent   market   store
where a conjurer calls
I possess what you yearn for
come   come

Behind a tent flap
beaded curtain   gilt door
some business   then
Kept just for you …

The sorcerer unfolds parchments
speaks as his finger traces
spells   rituals   studies
Light strikes potions in pots

She will carry her packages home
never forgetting
singing words   swaying steps

When she emerges
paparazzi will trail
reporters ask questions

She'll be beautiful but
start no Trojan wars

West End Afternoon

West End women with money
live apart   together
in high towers near parks
where elegant squirrels skirmish.

Japanese cherry in flower
pink as the small behind
of that white poodle
walking his mistress.

The large neutered cat on a bench
accepts adoration
from the woman beside him and

women
who are not Mrs. Robinsons
who did not coquettishly step
out of a Colette novel—
women who instruct young men
in the arts of love.

The bag lady downtown
who asked for pancake money
isn't shambling here.

ℰ
Daedalus's Daughter

Here's my realm
above   ahead   below

Can't stop you from staring but
stay behind that window

Told you
I'll leap at once
if you bring loved ones

Ahead   a bird
with his own agenda

Warm breeze
sun on my right
a perfect day to do something
Wish I had wings

Why don't you shut up?
I'm trying to think

Below—a crowd
urges me to join them
One holds up his boring camcorder
Haven't decided yet
whether to

JUMP! JUMP!

Skid Row

She didn't have much chance
worked too hard as a kid
Yelled at and beaten by parents
bullied by older kids
made to feel ashamed

Old men fingered her
crawled into her bed

She came to the city
was beaten to death
by this white guy
lived with her sometimes

They took care of everything
The nice young medical student
tenderly dissected the cold flesh

Elegy for Janis Joplin

They put me down, man, those square people ...
and I wanted them so much to love me. Janis Joplin

Uncantabile cries
From lips that were wet,
She swayed on the stage—
Playing Russian roulette?

Don't hold back the crowd,
They're my friends, doncha see?
They wanna dance close
And touch and feel me.

Her calls shook the hall,
Applause answered in air;
They said she had soul,
She whipped 'round her hair.

Back in a hotel
Needle in vein—
To help pass the time
Till she came live again?

A wish for you Janis—
Comfort somewhere,
In the arms of Bacchus
Feathered vines in your hair.

Did Anyone Hear?

Did anyone hear if
Safiya Husseini Tungar-Tudu
died today?

She was sentenced to death
to be buried in sand
up to her breasts and stoned

She had a baby out of wedlock
Judges granted her time after the birth
one hundred and forty-four days
to: reflect on her sins
while nursing her baby?

My breasts would've gone dry
just thinking about ...

Hearing—
the last sense to leave us
When dying, what would she hear

Did anyone hear
if Safiya died today?

*January 12, 2002 , was Safiya Husseini
Tungar-Tudu's execution date.*

I Scream, You Scream, Edvard

See the picture
dark as can be
see the artist
who painted it—me

What am I looking for?
What am I looking for?
A wall without a window
A house without a door

Program the rat
study the flea
condition the dog
and as for me

cut off my head
cut off my breasts
debone my body
dismember the rest

Quick! Nail down the coffin
throw the clay
raise a stone
tamp the turf
before I get away

History Lecture

The speaker brings his dog to the hall
She sits on the sidelines: quiet   alert
His lecture begins

Halfway through, the bitch whimpers softly
the speaker goes over, sees
blood on the floor
She raises a foot, he turns it over
The sole is slashed

To be here she has walked
on bleeding feet

Endangered Species

Breathless but ahead
she turns and waits
to fight the hunters

drops

licks blood from wounds
leans back into the vines
that mingle with her hair

dreams

thinks of others dead or caged
since so few like her are left
why this need to hunt her down

stirs

presses down ferns in front
wishes that she had some help
well they won't take her alive

listens

&.

Pawluv and Mawluv

Once the sciences of man were called behavioural sciences.

Pawluv and his assistant Mawluv
trained animals

Marker was their smartest dog
learned to salivate
when she wasn't hungry and
could push a button that stimulated
a pleasure center

No dropout
she wagged her tail at
figures labelled good and
attacked those labelled bad

Pawluv and Mawluv
pioneers in the sciences of man
worked with land mammals, then
went to the ocean and taught dolphins
to blow ships to the sky

where bright-eyed pigeons
strapped beneath planes
pecked buttons that activated bombs

Retired now
Pawluv and Mawluv
are confined in clean cubicles
Bells ring and they're
fed   washed   exercised
Don't see old pupils

Marker went to the dogs
They weren't taught
to love their trainers then

&

Down There

When Baby said *ears* they clapped hands with glee.
When she dropped panty and said *my wee-wee*
Heard, *Cover, touch to wash, and no abuse;*
Blindness and madness can follow such use.
Tried to keep mind off what I had down there
And when mother said *Wear clean underwear ...*
I thought if an accident left me a wreck,
Panty would be the first thing doctor'd check.

Once males stormed campuses on panty raids,
Held annual bare-butt Godiva parades.
A Granny who marched for peace overseas,
Squatted panty-less and raised skirt for pees.
Honouring women Judy Chicago
sculpted dishes and installed a show
Showing women's down theres on dinner plates.
Critics described it as different and great.

Tho' noble witches can revel sky clad
Dame Fashion once said seeing panty-line bad.
The most popular fashion show of our times—
The annual parade of new underwear lines.
Models in high heels strut as for lovers
In bits of fabric—such high-priced covers
For muff, naughty bits, crotch, vulva, hope chest,
Holy of holies, snatch, pussy—the rest.

Buyers wave orders for snippets and fluff—
Dylan said *Me and Marilyn don't wear the stuff.*

Fathers Lying in Our Depths like Fallen Mountains

from Rilke

*The death of someone with whom we have argued
violently throughout life is often a sad deprivation.*
Anthony Storr

In dreams on decks of sailing ships
My father found himself again,
On planking shined by holystones
He worked in sun, in wind, in rain.

All his life he kept his walk—
A sailor's sway, his pendulum roll,
His different drummer ocean-tuned,
He heard sea-rhythms in his soul.

And yes my father could be harsh,
Cold as a wind off Labrador;
Could still a young and noisy crew
Just by appearing at the door.

But Pisces had his other side—
He'd joke, tell tall tales, we had fun
And when he sang his Gaelic songs
He warmed my child-space like the sun.

When last we met we fought again,
I was unkind, purse-lipped and shrill.
He went into his yard and picked
Every in-bloom daffodil.

I boarded bus; he gave me them.
A foolish act I could have said
Before I ever reached my door
My mother's flowers would be dead.

From bus to taxi, boat to car,
I guarded them that awkward day;
And never thought to throw them in
A garbage can along the way.

Weeks later came a speeding truck
And he lay by the roadside dead.
I whisper, *Come back, I need you,*
Things are unsettled, things unsaid.

&

Monstrous Fact

The monstrous fact of children dying before their
parents ... Sigmund Freud

Mother is curled on top of the blankets
Saying over and over words that I dread.
I want to die, then her loud sobbing,
Why didn't he take me instead?

Mother, there were times we were not friendly;
Neither cared for the life the other one led.
But this is the fourth time you've opened a door
And been given the news, *Your child is dead.*

If it happened to me, a mother of four,
I would be childless—no step ahead.
Red-haired brother gone, oh I'll miss him longer—
Mothers, we weep and rock on the bed.

Extended Care

In memory of Winnifred Dorothy McLeod

Her arms empty now
no impatient child
no greedy lover
covets unclaimed breasts

She sleeps alone
kisses   endearments   stillborn
behind parted lips

Her floaty eyes
have life   still
something's sheared off

In the sun room
eyes skate off her
Her body embarrasses
coughing fits   rumblings
wind

Wets herself
lifts shaky legs into dry pants
shamed as a new-trained toddler
Forgets room number

Sometimes merry
tells   retells stories
those she knew when young

Quotes poets who
wrote verse in rhyme

Dream of an Old Waiting Room

There is a place I need to reach—
does a bus that can carry me there
stop here?

I sit on a bench in the almost empty
waiting room of an old bus stop
watch the silent man and woman
behind a counter occasionally go
to a chalky blackboard, rub something out
add smudged words, change columned numbers.

A small girl comes in the door—
yellow dress with a wide white collar
brown hair worn in a long Dutch bob
so full of radiant joy—
wish I'd been the child she is.

She comes to an older self
answers my unspoken question
puts warm arms around my neck
whispers clearly, *I love you.*

My body floods with such happiness—
I understand why saints bear what they do.

&

Adaptation

A marvel
no matter what happens
the body adapts
In spite of everything
somehow you grow

marry have sex
How belly swells—and
later you brush death
with birth

The body adapts
stretch marks fade
surplus skin shrinks
over the belly

Teeth are yanked out
dropped in a basin
(you know for a fact
you're not immortal)

Eyes
fitted with glasses
to which they adapt

Can a mind
childishly formed
ever adapt?

Politics of the Heart

Love is not what you think. Jessamyn West

If single
would I cry lonely
have body hungers   mouth   arms
longing for

whiskered face
Adam's apple   the urgent
damp shower smell

You said what I sometimes think
Like singed moths
words cripple the air

... *and unappreciative*

It's happened before   worse
rages   knee-capping words

Have we been together too long?
At our age we shouldn't
be acting like this
Stars burn out—life
is really too short now

We aren't locked in
There isn't
too much to settle
The children are grown
people have done it before
divided   I move
into the warm space you left
There must be bonds
even if we
don't call it love

Storms and Women

Thunder with his moving stirs / the brain ...
S.K. Heninger

Last night's storm
no namby pamby one

Not some picknose event
like fireworks before
Nanaimo's Bathtub Race

Shee-eet—at midnight
a thunderous racket
wild lightning to the horizon

Our storm—whacking off
light and decibels
would've done Jove proud or
turned him pea-green with envy

There were rains so heavy it seemed
every horse in the world was
pissin' over Nanaimo

Soldier Kruss you should'a been here
Coming home from war you said
Storms and women are
the best things in life
you shouldn't miss either

Near nine the jig was up and
there was enough blue
to make a Dutchman's britches

Moon Viewing

Moon's root of white crystal stretches toward the deep. Sumerian hymn

You fine female of a moon
a blind man could sense your stare

I watched you rise behind Gabriola Island
throw a molten track on the water
climb the Lombardy poplar—
fastigate branches fingered your face
before you mounted the southern sky
washing out stars in your wake

Now, ensconced in the west
you lightly nudge me
Don't sleep
Look at me   look at me

For goddess's sake go away
I bowed three times—
it's 3:00 a.m.   let me sleep

Years ago on a night bright as this
I sat on the Vancouver ferry
A friend of my husband's said
That's a marvellous moon—
like to stroll on the deck?

Oh-oo we needed
that thick pane of glass
between us and you

I was afraid if we went out
I might jump his beautiful bones

before the ferry reached the dock
where his wife
and my husband waited

I haven't seen you in years,
Madge says over coffee.
Remember Lily and Beth —
my two best friends?

I used to think some people
had cancer personalities.
Well —
Lily was diagnosed first,
had a double mastectomy
chemo ... radiation.
Six months later — Beth,
same surgery   same treatments.

I spent time with them
on the 5th floor, did what I could.
Lily, then Beth dead,
both exactly six months
after their diagnosis.

Sometimes I'm terrified.

I thought people
with cancer personalities
looked like the people
in American Gothic.

That woman in the painting:
hair in a bun, no makeup ...
She's not Lily or Beth.

Gotta run — I'm going to Vegas.
But you, how are you now?

Oh I'm feeling great, I say
people can survive. (a twinge of guilt)

Changing Woman

After her illness changing woman
moves through careful space
now knows the body can break
in places apart from the heart

Doctors and nurses crooned
over their needles and tubes
Amused she wanted to say
It's no use—I'm gone

She was trundled to isolation
Swaddled immigrants dropped in
moulted their white casings
just before leaving

Three weeks ticked away

Someone came back
to an estranged house
with an awkward kitchen

People around her seem
to want enthusiasm
Let her re-enter slowly
she's come from a long way away

Rain in the Morning

Six a.m.—evangelist crows
scream *You're headed for hell*
unless you get going.

Someone playing rock
slams his trunk twenty times
before he guns off.
A dog barks waking orders.

Listen: the thrum
of rain on the louvres.
Oh love
if we hadn't descended
from such a long line
of worker bees
we'd probably spend
this morning in bed ...

Your body   rises   falls
doing forty floor pushes.
I perform the right moves
in tai chi chuan.

Morning people   morning rain.

Alberta Game Farm in Winter

The leopard stares from a high platform
one elegant paw over the edge
Steve calls *Come down*

Small movements in chin and tail
What does she think of
my ten-year-old raising
his arms like an Olympic winner
Let's do something

Her bored stare   till he jogs
back and forth in front of her enclosure
then a bound—   and all
that dangerous beauty's beside him

He runs along the chain link fence
she passes him   waits at the end
He laughs   runs back
The cat wins so many times
he changes the rules   part way turns
runs the other way

How swiftly she catches on
to his broken-field running
Now he does Groucho Marx
makes a quick turnabout   another
Steve and this splendid prisoner
match steps in falling snow

He's flushed and sweating
she's lost none of her elegance
He wants to stay or return tomorrow
The last time he turns to wave
the leopard stares from her ledge

He will dream of bringing her home
of curling up beside her

Helen gives me the photo
her face half light   half darkness
Daughter you look so young, so sad.

That month I got about
two hours sleep a night
pulled all-nighters, took wake ups
wrote exams and essays.

An assignment:
make a shoe box camera.
No problem—she did that in grade five
but didn't take and finish
a photo from it then.

In neon night she prowled
Vancouver's seamier streets
looking for a model.

Then back in the dorm
from tired morning's mirror
Helen took herself.

৵

Grandchild

Child someday
I'll try to write
a poem about you

Anemone fingers search
Where is the warm pool
you recently lolled in?

Awake or sleeping
I love to look at
your dear newness

You have an aura
I am in awe
wanting you to not change

You do hourly

ॐ

On the Deck of the Shuddering Ferry

I watch drifting snowflakes
melt in steel grey waves

Two boys dawdle by—
from the back how like
the murderers we see
over and over
on the TV news

In an English mall
two school boys walk away
one holds a toddler's hand

Are the boys on this deck different
from the ten-year-old kids who battered
life from a small child's body?

It's so cold—I'll get a coffee
forget that my two-year-old grandson
will go with anyone

Bring snacks from Lethe, let the children forget
Violence that surrounded, how they were beset.
Transform the horror held in their young heads,
Hug them and tuck them in warm soft beds.

Let beds be on barges to be poled away
To a safe harbour where children can play.
Cared for by tellers of old tales who mime,
Start stories beginning *Once upon a time.*

No fists, boots, belts, sticks to frighten those here,
This haven where small ones are cared for and dear.
Somewhere on a shore, where the sea-flowers creep,
Let a snuggle of children drift sweetly to sleep.

Visitant

Friends are building
on Gabriola Island
the house smells of woods
not of a family

We're surprised
how large the home they're building
when all but one son's gone
How much land does a man need
How much house a woman

She says it's an investment
he talks retirement

Their teenage son shows
a human skull he found
in a nearby midden

Quiet midnight
we hear tapping in the basement
where doors are yet unhung

Peer down the stairs
There! In the flashlight's beam
an island deer
staring back at us

Beacon Hill Peacocks

Fine to be that peacock
strutting in sumptuous colours
step - step - turn
He knows cameras are on

White among the scrub
disconsolate by the board fence
an albino peacock
Paled Argus eyes
haunt

You're rare but
where's whiteness got you —
the cold periphery

Do the flock judge it deliberate
think you choose not to be normal
like him — who's having such a good time
followed by scuttling females?

If albino, be something cute —
like a hummingbird or
grow grandiose, be Moby Dick

Change sex — nothing's
expected of peahens
You're like some illustration
in a paint-by-numbers book
I long for crayons
to fill in all that whiteness

I SPRING

Lord this is a huge rayn! Chaucer

Old rain
you don't need words to din
All is water into my body

Want to return me to earth
only trees are at ease
in this magic rainforest

I shelter beneath a large fir
press back into bark
You'll come to me yet

Puddle home where radio
can't drown rain sound
You are part of what is outside

Oh watery wasteland where
it raineth every day—or threatens
rain   not violets

Slides block roads   cars
like stranded whales
Night rain loud

Curl in the foetal position
Lord this is a huge rayn!
This were a weder for to slepen inn!

II SUMMER

There is no rain here to make one reflective.
Lawrence Durrell

One clear and clever Houdini night
clouds disappear   procrastinating
sunshine dumbfounds dulled eyes

Join in the flow of bodies from buildings
lift worshipping arms
face up-tilted gulp down light

Dream kid dreams of tans & convertibles
dawdle through beatific days
soundly sleep under alphabet stars

III AUTUMN

O, rain, be merciful.
Wash away the sharp edges of the world.
Katherine Anne Porter

Some rainforest autumns
the incongruous sun
hangs on too long

Mythic salmon who swim obsessed
toward their natal stream
find birth creek dry

Throng-thrashing they move
Oh rain you are late
these fish cannot spawn

Hydrophilic—I'm disoriented
long with trees that belong
for rain   to wash and freshen

bring its greeny odours
No *gentle rain from heaven*
a real pour of rain

IV Winter

Silent snow, secret snow. Conrad Aiken

One drape-pulling morn
there's seldom-come-snow
in our rainforest

A black dog in whiteness
rompingly runs—cellular memories
of pulling a sled?

A fallen child creates an angel
Wrapped school's-out children
craft snowmen and forts

Aware—I'm a Canadian
P.E.I. to V.I.   bones of my kin
dream beneath all the snow

I drive like a drunk—an Easterner nags
Carry a shovel and sand in your car
Thought I knew my place

Even birds are confused
when snow-laden branches on conifers crack—
furtive eyes search for suitable green

Neanderthal nose tests air for rain—
spent by shovelling I burrow in blankets
a dance of rain   permeating my dream

Like a soiled trollop snow sloppily leaves
I can write in this light
let it rain   let it rain

The Wintering Land

In the city cemetery
an angel on a pedestal
turns her back to me
gazes at the sea

the pulp mill squeezes smoke
along the waterfront

Nanaimo's storied high-rises
built on plundered land

   loom

  phallic in fog

Old-timers have predicted
they will sink or topple

The wintering land waits
for the return of gifts

Frozen Seas

Our frozen northern seas
calve islands of ice.
One stares at me.

Behind the ship's rail
I'm drawn into the gaze
of an untamed animal
into whose space
I have fecklessly trespassed.

Eyes—jagged crystals—warn
I could kill you.

The captain states
We aren't too close
even if that baby rolls over
what's hidden won't touch us.

Holes: An Introductory Lecture

Anyone who assumes I'll talk
of small hollows in which balls are put
or bodily orifices, including those classified as
Naughty Bits, may leave

This is a whole other subject of deep
sometimes dark, interest to humans—
excavations in landscapes

Observations:
For several days in a neighbour's yard
a golden bulldozer has repeatedly raised
its hinged neck then dropped it
so its nearly all-mouth head can bite the earth
Is it the machine or a pheromone
from the hole that attracts males?
They stand respectfully in light rain
observing the hole deepen

I never joined the watchers; it's just
my kitchen windows look across the alley
and into this neighbour's back yard

For days I saw a dirt mound grow
concluded there was a sunken hole
of similar mass in my neighbour's lot

This will only be an introduction to
a deeper study on cavities in our planet
An internet search will doubtless bring up
studies by people who've dug much deeper—
have degrees in Psychology or Bulldozing
or the Psychology of Bulldozing
There may even be an anthology on holes
published by Rundown House or somesuch

This evening, if the gazers have gone
and my neighbour is staring into his excavation
I may walk by and say hello—could bring him
a nice bit of toad in the hole

Drive in a Prairie Set

I was born
in homestead country, now
Island-transplanted eyes
view this place

A speeding pilgrim
I can remember wading
in ankle-deep black loam
the way my children waded
in Parksville's shallow waters

Drive. Notice clouds, sky
the torn-paper horizon
Feel like a child
given a prairie play set—
such absorbing pieces

On the patchwork base
there's a green field for
this man on a tractor

Place a silo
next to the new red barn
This is the deluxe set
it has an old barn too
a garish green new farmhouse
and a crumbling grey one

Put a slough there
I made mud pies by one
trying to escape
summer's heavy heat
under shady poplars

Pieces are missing
the one-room schoolhouse

dad helped to build
on land he'd donated

Horses—don't see Nancy
the mare he loaned
to the from-east teacher
so she could ride to school

Make a pretty picture
put an old white church
in grass and buttercups
here off the highway
pretend they married there

Place dipping bird oil rigs
here and there on flatland
Put up some signage

SLOWER TRAFFIC KEEP RIGHT

RURAL CRIME WATCH

BLIND MAN RIVER

Drive
behind Big Horn Transport
through wild rose country

Some things are familiars
crows   mailboxes
yellow school busses
an auto graveyard
CBC radio

Drive by MORNINGSIDE
as Peter's guest says
... *we all have scars*

Should I stop
in some town with
a store, dim beer parlour
where the local band
plays Wilf Carter music?

DO NOT CROSS MEDIAN

Drive, rush home to smaller skies
scissored by peaks
The glacial mountains
jut like locomotives

Ixtapa: What Are the Waves Saying?

Each hour of Ixtapa's twenty-four
We watch, are watched, as waves break on the shore.
Slim vendors stalk the borders of this beach:
Brown, barefoot, burdened, under sun's hot reach.

A fisherman in water first-rib high,
Throws his small circle net into the sky.
Deaf to my pale-skinned curiosity
Tosses again—draws quivering life from sea.

Gaunt women hawk, *Look lady! Almost free!*
The restless gleam of silver circles me.
While tourists haggle over crafted rings
Someone on knees cuts lawn—machete swings.

The native children trudge while tourists play,
Our white room spotless—bed made twice a day.
Great blue-green waves crash down upon the shore,
We're sun-drenched, cozened, that's what we came for.

Blind in the Sun

The blind woman sits
at a patio table
dappled in sun
An unpetted cat
purrs into her skirt
Neither objects to
my trespassing eyes

Wouldn't stare
like this at home
Here I'm a tourist
pretending to write
postcards to friends
while others day tour

She isn't deaf—
turned to the screen door
when the no-nonsense woman
who runs the café
came out with a baby

A few unheard words
then child is placed
in the blind woman's lap

Ah—this is better
is there a story?
Are these two sisters?
Who's mother and who
has fathered the baby?

Not that old man
pulling leaves over tiles

Nothing is happening
Blind woman show me
how lacking one sense
you're twice blessed in others
Let your trailing fingers
trace baby's face   sniff
nuzzle   talk nonsense
croon some sweet folk song
while rocking or nursing

Why don't I go over
say *Your baby's lovely*
Her answers will tell me
if it's boy or girl and ...

Tonight at table
while others are chatting
of views and statues
I'll have a story

Maybe illicit
as is good gossip
or worth writing up
when I'm back home

(behind the screen door
someone's dark shadow)

These people will live here
when tour's gone tomorrow
I'm tourist   not pilgrim
just one more writer
(a second-hand human)
with ink on my breath
trying to sell somebody out

§◆

Spring 2000 in Halifax

Halifax ... the place periodically sleeps between
great wars. Hugh MacLennan

My parents lived here once. I've never been here before
unless you count time I was in mother's clutch of eggs

Halifax, 1917, she waited
for the war to end all wars to end

I search old streets for the place
where she rented housekeeping rooms
when dad was mine-sweeping

Don't know its address, was it like this place
bordered with old-fashioned flowers, or that one there?
You can't find a house destroyed in the explosion

I enter an old park where mother wheeled ten-month-old Hector
while two-year-old Freida held onto the pram's handle

On this path beneath a bare tree there's a smashed egg
with an embryonic something. Stare up—there's no nest
Where did it come from? and
this shard from a blue willow plate
a pattern mother loved

I worry the shard in my pocket
as I walk toward the water
through space thick with history

The End of the Trail in Trail

Each urn held what was once a person ...
We wanted to give them rest, dignity, closure.
Funeral Director

They did a good thing in Trail
held a funeral service
for seventy-six people

Their unclaimed ashes were stored
some almost three score years

A choir sang at their rites
the pastor gave a eulogy
all recited the Lord's Prayer
for the casket of cremains

Someone told a reporter
he wasn't a relative but
knew one of the guys—*a loner*
seemed nice, maybe drank too much
worked with him in the smelter

&
Documentary

You Aran Islanders
your courage haunts

Shawled and stoic women
knitting family crests
into sturdy sweaters

If brother   lover   son
is lost beneath the waves
his body washed
into some strange tide-pool

they know who to send for
by the pattern knit
into his warm wool sweater

Elderberry Wine

He dreamed of being wed
to an old-fashioned girl
happy with broom and pots

Married her all in white
The church was full of strangers
he was related to

Something old were her ways
he was the bridegroom, new
her veil was borrowed
his eyes were blue

The preacher left early—
something to do with her saying
she believed older books

Handy with a needle
she tattooed a rose on his breast
sewed him a tam with a feather
and a jewelled codpiece

Their double bed was circled
by five-gallon crocks
full of burbling juice
Herbs hung from ceilings

He left her woods one morning
moved to a high-rise with
his indexed pension

He missed elderberry wine
She missed seeing him
knew spells to bring him back
a curse to set him wasting

What is the sound
of one hand clapping?

Is it something like:
the sound of dew falling
    a tulip opening
    a cherry ripening
    grapes swelling
of green leaving the poplars
a leaf in the wind or the sound
of an old car rusting?

Or is it something like
the sound of the sun setting
the sound of the stars coming?

Old Norse God Hamdal
could hear the grass growing
Did he know the sound
of one hand clapping?

The Children of the Man in the Moon

The children of
the man in the moon
are close to their mother
Their father goes off
as soon as he finds
she's pregnant
again

The children have eyes
like Orphan Annie's
Go to school
as required   leave
as soon as they're able
At recess they huddle
    watching the way
    children play

Live on a farm
mostly woods   has sea frontage
Their dogs descended from wolves
The children of
the man in the moon
have eyes like deep water

Long-haired and
barefoot in summer
they come to town
with berries and baskets
cascara bark
driftwood and oysters
all kinds of mushrooms

Don't know what religion
they follow — if any
sometimes hear singing
more of a chant

The children of
the man in the moon
have eyes like chameleons'

Rejection Mountain

Wolves came down a mountain to a river. They
swam across. On the way over their fur began to
fall out. When they reached land their hides were
smooth. They scrambled up the bank, found they
could balance on their hind legs. They opened their
mouths to howl and guttural sounds came forth.
They were the first people.

Don't come to the mountain alone
it's never been mapped completely

The largest wolves in the world—
somebody snapped them once
found his film exposed

If you must climb here
stay within sight of a partner
be down before it gets dark

The North Face avoids the sun
surly mist has settled
dis-eased by our presence

Here decay comes swiftly
Pick up a leaf new-fallen
already it feels slimy

They still talk of logging
all the machinery damaged
and the men who were maimed

Keep your voices down
why rouse anything sleeping
People have died on the mountain

Remember the lost housewife?
Found her way down the North Face
looked in her lighted windows

re-climbed the mountain
They followed her tracks at daybreak
clothing scattered like leaves
stones grouped around her

Something gets to its feet
don't walk so far from me
I want to be out of these wolf woods
I want to be down the mountain

֍

For the Celtic Goddess Cerridwen

*Her name means cauldron, her brew causes
one to burst into prophecy, poem or song.*

To cauldron come
bring something with you
to stir into song

Honey and nuts
barley   bull's blood
three Bee-sisters come

Take of it   make
something of it
a handle-less poem

turn like a Gypsy
reading the leaves
you don't need leaves

see-er   self seer

River is lake
is cauldron
is cup

ﻬ

From Her Fingers Came Thousands of Singing Birds

from a poem by Mildred Tremblay

She let
imagination wing
Made

owls with wise eyes
hammer-headed woodpeckers
nutcracker-jawed parrots
long-billed curlews
eagles with unforgiving eyes

Made birds in song shapes
air-anchored hummers — gave
grace to swift and swallow
loon a call to haunt twilights
Such perfect design

Then She heard what
Audubon's Lucy would cry
In every bird I have a rival!

So She made some for fun —
rhinoceros hornbills —
gave peacock a fishwife voice
invented a waddle of penguins

Then:
the loud-mouthed crows
who like to live easy
hang out in groups
cause trouble

A Net to Catch Stars

I'm tatting a net to catch stars
the mesh could be finer
smaller ones may slip through

Thought I'd try the ocean first
there must be thousands of
fallen stars just floating there
ready to be raked in—
wiped and varnished and
printed with something nice
Waste Not Want Not
Souvenir of Nanaimo

I can't lose—I'll
hawk them at bazaars
sell them in shoppes
tourists'll grab 'em

First I'll finish this net to catch stars

Letters to Poets

Tranced mendicants stare at taper
They wait with pen and empty paper

Dear Marianne Moore:
How your phrase made mind inroads
imaginary gardens with real toads

Dear Obscure Poet:
You whisper and you shout—
but whatinhell are you talking about?

Dear Young Poet:
In your poems you write the truth
although you're barely past your youth

Dear Sylvia:
At retreating backs you yelped
somebody should have helped

Dear Stanley Cooperman:
You wrote poems and some were fun
you put down pen, picked up a gun

Dear Auden: The kindest thing is not to live too long you said
Maybe you're right—but you can't write when you're dead

Dear Fellow Sinners:
Sometimes I think poets bent over their pages
are like saints muttering from the stone ages

On the Centennial of Hemingway's Birth

People you read about constantly have a transcendental
quality ... when they die a piece of your personal experience
dies with them. Charles Harris

Black ice pitched me down steps and broke my arm,
Hand rigid end of cast, I cannot write,
Had it been left limb would have done less harm.

Some think a flow goes to right hand through arm,
From head to hand that scribes our thoughts on white.
Black ice pitched me down steps and broke my arm.

Once tomboy, I broke nothing on our farm.
How hard my landing and so brief my flight,
Had it been left limb would have done less harm.

My writing tap's off, can't dismay or charm,
Sleep sitting up—keep bone alignment right.
Black ice pitched me down steps and broke my arm.

Some believe blocked words no cause for alarm.
Early at desk to work his sacral rite,
Had it been left limb would have done less harm.

Took an expedient gun, raised no alarm—
Saw writing on the wall, had sad foresight?
Black ice pitched me down steps and broke my arm,
Had it been left limb would have done less harm.

Poet

She praises his work
He asks her
to do his laundry

Reads a tender poem
about his daughter—mauls teenagers
at his reading

Tells her he loves her—
he'll write a sad poem
when he leaves

A poet is someone who writes
no matter what
May be myopic
yet see afar

If she says she loves you
remember—before she had good sense
she fell in love with words
still is married

Learn this: she
will use you
vacillate about causes
already has a cause

Knows what she'd save
from burning buildings
Don't expect her
if she hears a poem

&.

The Wind Has Words for Us Too

from Donald James

While her lover slept in the dawn
a woman hung clothes in the garden
Something in bird talk
the way the apple tree whispered
warned a wind of words was near

She darted in for a pillow-slip
gathered from the twirl
words whirling about

Caught what she could
slammed them into her sack
No reading first to ponder
should she take this one   that
She'd learned the wind could leave
before you'd gathered enough

Higgledy-piggledy stuffed
booty into her bag
When it overflowed
she put words in pockets
pencil behind ear
hair in pits, *nipple* in bra

Greedy for words
she caught *bread* in her teeth then
bent with her bounty she staggered in

Spilled
the amniotic sac
of so many words
over the table, some
fell to the floor

She cleared a space
began her mosaic

Her lover came scratching in—
wanted food and love
he carelessly walked on a word
She took wood and
whacked him out the door
turned key in lock

Quickly selected words
jig-sawed into place
she slid them on paper

Words shifted
slipped out of the template
slid off the page

She tossed them in air
they came down right—but there
were spaces for missing words
Found one in her pocket
one in her head just waiting
one in the load of laundry
forgotten in the garden

When she took the hoe
from her lover's hands
he nimbly climbed
into apple boughs
She took thyme and went inside

Patted words in place
then read her poem aloud
for meanings behind words
Does not the ear try words
as the palate tastes food?

She returned to the garden, shook
unused words into the wind
Her lover leaped from the apple tree—
she opened her arms, caught love

The Mad Woman's Song

A mad woman sings by the side of a road,
A mad woman sways and rattles her gourd.

Have you seen my head? I lost it some place,
Two eyes, two ears in their usual place,
A nose for the breath and ears for the sound,
Had hair back and sides and was somewhat round.

And oh how the words grew in it when young,
Some stayed in their place some flowed from the tongue.
Some brought smiles to others when said,
Some brought me looks you'd give folk you'd like dead.

By scoldings and smackings learned laws and rules,
Was conscious of power at home and in schools.
Looking for answers read thousands of tales,
Histories and poems, written mostly by males.

In churches my ears took drilling words in
Black suits explained what was pleasing to men.
Father to husband from no duty fled,
Mind-numbing work felled me thoughtless in bed.

Four children arrived, raised boy, boy, girl, boy,
I should have paused then to savour the joy.
It was do this, go there—no, no time to play.
Those small bodies grew, waved and walked away.

Booze was no answer, though first it sang fine,
Women thought waving drowned in cups like mine.
Shall I join Keats' robin out on some sill?
Find me a wild wood, where tall trees grow still?

A mad woman sings near the end of the road,
An Ophelia who survived, grey as a toad.

Metamorphosis

I'm busy
growing my new skin

Takes some doing
lack method and practice

I'm stumbly-bumbling
learning as I grow

Unlike some creatures
won't emerge in younger garb

My new skin will be older, wrinkled
but comfortably mine

No can't—am busy
growing my new skin

Long Time Married

You sleep on your left side
forearm under my forearm
our hands matched

Time I got going
but won't chance waking you
What's better than being here?

Finally you can dream
after your night of sore bones
You mutter, *I'll keep you warm*

A sciatic tremor—do your legs ache from:
that old soccer injury
falling with the extension ladder
trying to jump as high as a grandkid
kicking the fence posts down when
a sledgehammer's smack didn't do it?

Daft—
to think you would go gentle
into the good night.

Autumnal

I Goose Summer Dawn

Everything's golden: low clouds
teasled above the horizon,
sky, ocean, street, pears and
the droughty lawn still damp
from last night's rain.

I never thought April cruel,
September seems more so
withdrawing its light from flowers
whispering de la Mare's words
Look thy last on all things lovely.

Age's inexorable trap
seventy Septembers
celled in my bones

Caught in this frangible body
faculties shearing off
will I come to believe Hagiwara
*Who grown old can look
in a true mirror without horror?*

Should age be a foreboding thing?
Seek beauty, can this season bring
consolations for no longer being forty?

Honour this older woman.
You are here now,
eat an orange and read the paper.

There's even a bird singing
in the amber dawn.

II STILL DAYLIGHT SAVINGS TIME

... withering, preparing to go back to earth and stars.
Chrystos

Whitman wrote of age's grandeur
but we don't believe an old person
is a rare jewel. Unlike some old buildings
old women are not revered.

Should age be an anathema
if I'm not afraid of death?
It doesn't come alone.

Once a child's cries reeled me to a crib
I'd nurse a hungry baby
muse how great it would be
someday to sleep in.

Children gone but
I still wake at nun's hours.

Face it—Nature doesn't need me
but I haven't been marooned
to drift away on an ice floe.
I'm not—not yet anyway
a grown child's nightmare:
a fetid body in grungy clothes
whiskered and mumbling
over meals of tea and toast.

Warm baths, good food, soft sleep, and generous wine
These are the rights of age, and should be thine.

Homer, I want something more,
not to become unselved.

The Fleshes

She stood at the open closet
Looking at her pretty dresses;
Remembering him, his happy singing,
Oh the fleshes! Oh the fleshes!

She'd straightened dress and grammar
After lifting back her tresses:
Say 'oh the flesh' or 'pretty breasts',
Not 'Oh the fleshes, Oh the fleshes'.

A house was calling, calling her
From woods not made for dresses
So she left him and his magic,
Oh the fleshes! Oh the fleshes!

Why are they hanging there?
They no longer fit—those dresses
That covered up her body,
All her fleshes, oh the fleshes!

ﾞ➍
Acknowledgements

Thanks to the editors of the following
anthologies and publications in which many of
these poems originally appeared:

ANTHOLOGIES

After the Eclipse, Alberta Poetry Yearbooks
(Canadian Authors' Association, 1982, 88),
Classical Antiquity—A Modern Odyssey,
Doors of the Morning, Panty Lines: A Poetic
Anthology (Blue Moon Press, 2000), *From this*
New World (Ten Dollar Words, 2003), *Here*
is a Poem (League of Canadian Poets, 1983),
The Invention of Birds (Leaf Press, 2003), *No*
Love Lost (Hidden Brook Press, 1998), *Love*
in Four Positions (Leaf Press, 2002), *To an*
Inland Sea, The Wisdom of Old Souls (Hidden
Brook Press, 2008), *Witness to Wilderness: The*
Clayoquot Sound Anthology (Arsenal Pulp
Press, 1994).

JOURNALS

Ariel, Art Counselor, BC BOOKS, Bird Verse
Portfolios, Bogg, Broomstick, Canadian
Women's Studies, Canadian Bulletin of
Medical History, Canadian Writers' Journal,
Crone Chronicles, CVII, Discovery, Ego
Rag, Elder Statesman, Green's Magazine,
Herizons, Herspectives, HWUP!, Impetus,
Life on Earth, Living Message, Malaspina
Review, Museletter, New Quarterly—Special
Issue Family Fictions, Northwest Magazine,
Owlflight, Palomar Showcase, Penumbra,
Pierian Spring, Pioneer News, Poemata,
Portal, Poetry USA, Raincoast, Rainforest,
Room of One's Own, Seaside Woman,
Shorelines, SWAG, Western People, Whetstone.

Born on March 18, 1924, in Southey,
Saskatchewan, into a large family, Winona
Louise Baker moved to B.C. in 1930. Living
in Nanaimo, she raised four children with her
husband Art. A Haiku specialist, she received
the top global prize in a 1989 World Haiku
Contest in honour of Matsuo Basho's 300th
anniversary. After self-publishing with Red
Cedar Press, she released *Moss-Hung Trees*
with Gabriola's Reflections Press. It takes
its title from her prize-winning haiku. Her
other books include *Beyond the Lighthouse*
(Oolichan, 1992) and *Even a Stone Breathes*
(Oolichan, 2000).

In 1994 the Romanian Haiku Society gave
her a Commemorative Medal and in 1997 an
Award of Excellence for her paper presented
at a Symposium on Basho in Bucharest. The
Croatian Haiku Association also presented her
with an award in 1997.

Winona Baker's work is in more than seventy
anthologies in North America, New Zealand,
Japan and Europe, including *The Haiku
World: An International Poetry Almanac*
(Kodanshu International 97: 621 poets from
52 countries writing in 25 languages), and has
been translated into Japanese, French, Greek,
Croatian, Romanian, Yugoslavian. She has
haiku in *The Book of Hope,* an international
anthology published to raise funds for children
in Afghanistan. Her work is archived in the
Haiku Museum, Tokyo; the Basho Museum,
Yamagata; the American Haiku Archives in
California, and the Haiku Collection in the
Fraser-Hickson Library Montreal.